Finding Your Fire & Keeping It Hot

Discovering Your Why, Your Passion, Your Purpose in Life

Diana Stout, MFA, Ph.D.

This book cannot be reproduced or used without expressed written permission from the author with the exception of a review.

All rights reserved.

Cover design by
Nancie Rowe Janitz Designs
Sharpened Pencils Productions LLC

Copyright © 2022 Diana Stout, MFA, PhD

All rights reserved.

ISBN-13: 978-0-9974223-8-2

DEDICATION

To all those individuals who have fed my fire and encouraged me along the way. I hold you dear in my heart.

Also by Diana Stout

Grendel's Mother
Determined Hearts
Shattered Dreams: A Laurel Ridge Novella (#1)
David & Goliath
"Maggie's Story"
The Super Simple Easy Basic Cookbook
Tomorrow's Wish for Love
Love's New Beginnings
Lost and Found – romance anthology

CONTENTS

Also by Diana Stout iv
Acknowledgements ix
Introduction – Read Me First! 1
Part I: Who, What, Where, & Why 5
   Chapter 1: What & Where Is the Fire? 7
   Chapter 2: Why Fires Are Needed & Desired 11
   Chapter 3: Who Has the Fire? 13
   Chapter 4: What is True Success? 17
      Success Assignment 22
   Chapter 5: What's Your *Why*? 23
      Passion Assignment 24
      Why Assignment 27
   Chapter 6: What's Your Passion Quotient? 29
      Passion Quotient Evaluation Assignment 30
Part II: Universal Laws 33
   Chapter 7: Important Universal Laws 35
      The Law and Principle of Time 35
      Law of Polarity 36
      Law of Abundance 37
      Law of Action 38
      Law of Attraction 39
      Law of Vibration 42

    Law of Karma 44

Part III: Finding Your Fire 49
    Chapter 8: Discovering Your Fire.............................51
        Discovery Assignment 52
    Chapter 9: Making a Decision...................................55

Part IV: Now What?...59
    Chapter 10: Making a Plan 61
    Chapter 11: Setting Goals 63
    Chapter 12: Building Your Fire Properly 65
    Chapter 13: Helping Your Subconscious 69

Part V: When the Fire Dies..73
    Chapter 14: How Fires Die 75
        Worry, Anxiety, Stress Assignment 78
    Chapter 15: Writer's Block..85

Part VI: Restarting Your Fire 87
    Chapter 16: Making Changes....................................89
    Chapter 17: Restarting Your Fire..............................99

Part VII: Protecting Your Fire................................... 101
    Chapter 18: Why Your Fire Needs Protection 103
    Chapter 19: Dealing With Regrets..........................109

Part VIII: The Final Test.. 113
    Chapter 20: Final Assignment.................................115
    Chapter 21: In Conclusion 119

About the Author 121
Can You Help Me, Please? 122
Coming soon! 123

ACKNOWLEDGEMENTS

A special thanks to my Brainstorming Babes who kept prodding and pushing me to start my series of how-to books, this one as the first in the series. And, a special thank you to the members of MMRWA who were equally encouraging in my writing these helpful how-to books.

Finding Your Fire & Keeping It Hot

INTRODUCTION – READ ME FIRST!

So, why am I sharing my journey of my fire with you?

It's because I discovered my fire was my *Why*, the reason I was put on this earth. To not share would be to devalue my *Why*.

I want you to find your fire and enjoy its journey as enthusiastically as I have mine and for you to discover that you can fulfill that seemingly impossible dream.

Earlier in life, I envied those people who had found their life's passion while young: the singers, pianists, guitarists, golfers, fashion designers, entrepreneurs, ice skaters, and so many other fields.

I've especially envied the writers who not only found their genre early but became a high-ranking best-selling authors in the process, as well.

That's not to say that these writers found financial success early, but their passion for writing kept them determined and dedicated.

I found walking with determination and dedication as I journeyed with my fire served me well.

It's those characteristics—determination and dedication—that can enable you to succeed in your desire to pursue your passion.

Writing is my fire and has been my passion for over forty-five years.

When I was fifteen in tenth grade, that's when I saw that first spark, a spark that lasted about the length of a match burning.

At nineteen, another spark flickered, this one becoming a small flame, but it too went out after just a few months.

Then suddenly, in my mid-20s, that flame lit up again, only this time I began writing diligently, which led to my feeding the fire regularly and getting published.

My fire has become a culmination of serving through teaching and writing. It took me a long time to realize they needed to be paired up together.

Part I of this book assumes you haven't found your passion yet, the thing that fires up your creativity, your desire to work on a project or perform an activity outside of work and family. Part I will help you understand the drive behind a fire, why it's needed, and help you determine the level of success you will want to achieve.

More importantly, you'll be able to uncover your *Why*—the reason why you're here.

Part II of this book explains the unseen science and vibrational energy that drive various universal laws that work for us or against us in positive or negative ways, respectively. As you became cognizant of these laws at work and seeing them in action, you'll be watching magick in motion.

Part III provides activities to help you discover your true fire. You may discover, as I did, that you have many interests, many passions, but only one is your true fire, the passion that answers the questions: *Why am I here? What is my purpose in life?*

Part IV is for those who have found their fire but don't know what to do with it.

Part V shows how our fires can die or become diminished, how you may be killing your fire without realization.

Part VI shows you how to get your fire back.

Part VII is about how to safeguard and protect your fire, how you can keep it burning bright, and contains the concluding summary, along with your take-away from the assignments and challenges I offer you.

Because I'm a writer, my examples in this book will generally be about writing and writers. However, you can take any field and apply my message and examples to your desired field while trying to find your fire.

My wish is that you will find this process of finding your fire and keeping it burning bright as magical as I did.

Part I: Who, What, Where, & Why

"If you change the way you look at things, the things you look at change."

– Wayne Dyer

DIANA STOUT

CHAPTER 1: What & Where Is the Fire?

Fire. A basic, natural element that our early ancestors discovered, which prolonged their lives by providing heat, light, safety, security, a signal, and as a home hearth even if home was a cave.

The fire I'm talking about has some of those same qualities, but this fire is the passion that burns within each of us.

For some, this fire is merely a small light—like that of a match. You see or feel glimpses of it but then it's gone. For others, that fire is a lone coal—a remnant from a once flaming, hot log-filled fire where the coals are still warm. You just don't know what to do with it or how to get the coal(s) to flame again. For others still, that fire was flaming hot and then burned out completely and you want it back.

This inner fire is our desire that makes us feel alive, gives meaning to our lives. The more we work with that fire, the more fuel we're adding to it, which further builds our passion for it. Even when we're only thinking about it.

For some people this fire is their career, for others it's their volunteer work. For others still, it's doing something creative or being active in a sport.

The common denominator for all of these people is that their fire is self-satisfying and self-fulfilling.

According to Maslow's Hierarchy of Needs[1] chart below, when we're working with our fire and passion, we're in the top tier of Self-Actualization Needs, the level of self-fulfillment. As you can see by the size of each level, there will be fewer people operating in the top self-actualization level than are living and operating in the various lower levels.

Your fire's purpose can involve activities located anywhere on the ladder. And, it's possible to move up and down the ladder because of sudden, unexcepted circumstances. But once you've been at the top of the ladder, it's easy to return to the top.

Only a small portion of the world's population reach the self-actualization level. Many people spend their entire day surviving, living at the bottom three levels their entire lives.

---

[1] Psychologist Abraham Maslow created a hierarchy of needs, all driven by human motivations of unsatisfied needs and desired needs, and the philosophy that lower hierarchy needs have to be satisfied before higher needs can be addressed.

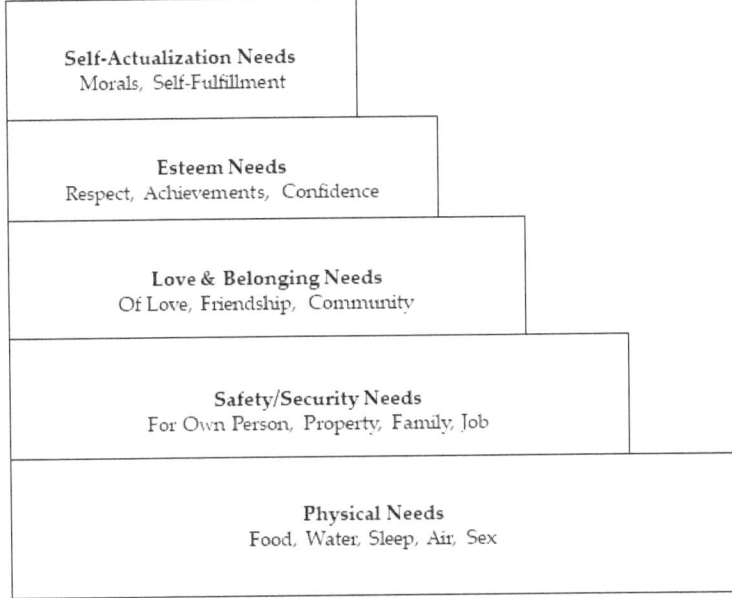

Many people tend to believe that life's purpose is to be happy.

Actually, happiness is a byproduct of our actions — not of what we purchase or in what we accumulate.

While many believe relationships can make them happy, true happiness comes not from others but from within. Relationships *enhance* what is already within, good or bad. That said, should your fire be about serving others whether through family or elsewhere, that service measured by your level of happiness is the result of doing and how you tend to the fire within.

Our fire can serve others or it can serve ourselves, providing us the ability of expression. There are no rules or boundaries on what our fire must be. Each fire is an original outcome of that individual's core.

So, where are you on Maslow's Hierarchy? Are you trying to find your way to the Self-Actualization level but aren't sure how to get there?

This book will help you achieve that goal.

CHAPTER 2: Why Fires Are Needed & Desired

The fires we have within operate the same way a hearth fire operates.

Our early ancestors used fire for cooking, protection, light, making tools, and recreation as they gathered around it, planning, and telling stories.

Fire was an important element of their existence. Likewise, finding our fire, our passion within is equally important.

Our fire feeds us by giving our lives meaning.

Our fire keeps the feelings of despair away. It warms us with self-fulfillment and self-satisfying moments of our achievements.

Our fire provides us with an inner light, providing our lives with positivity.

Our fire provides a cleansing against the mental infection of dissatisfaction.

And, our fire provides us with motivation to keep taking steps forward, allowing us to see our growth of empowerment, giving us the belief that we can achieve our desires.

Returning to Maslow's Hierarchy of Needs . . .

Someone who is seeking to fulfill their basic physical needs because of their community's situation or a disaster of nature, isn't going to be seeking out the upper layers of fulfillment. It's all they can do to find food, water, a place to sleep. Usually, these are temporary situations or conditions, not life-long events.

Sometimes in trying to overcome a past where a lower need suffered, an upper activity can be used. For example, someone who suffered abuse at the hands of a family member (Safety/Security) could write a memoir (Self-Actualization, Esteem), allowing them to put the past behind them.

The point I'm making is that the handicaps of life do not have to diminish your fire. It's natural to go up and down Maslow's Ladder due to circumstances and even daily events. And, it's possible to reside in more than one level of that ladder at a time.

CHAPTER 3: Who Has the Fire?

Look around you.

Everyone has an inner fire but you wouldn't know it by looking at them. For some, while they may have a passion they engage in, that passion hasn't been lit yet.

Others may be frustrated, not knowing how to change their lives so that they can engage with their fire.

There are some who are content with their lives but still feel like something is missing.

And then, there are those who have a fire going, which you may know nothing about, and they're not only content but happy.

Too often we judge another's happiness by external conditions, such as by their job, their home, or the neighborhood in which they live.

So what if that person doesn't have what you deem as the best job and lives in less than desirable home or neighborhood? If that person is genuinely happy that's all that matters. Some people choose to spend their money on experiences rather than big homes they can barely afford or maintain. I prefer renting small apartment because I've needed to be free to move without a hassle, plus I want to keep my footprint small. For me, less has been more. Also, I lived small so that I could become debt-free from my college and car loans quickly, while still investing in my writing.

A truly happy person pursuing their passion doesn't have regrets. Oh, they may have wished for different outcomes at different earlier times, but overall, there are no regrets. They understand that the trials and tribulations of earlier times molded them into what they are today.

Having a fire, having that passion provides you with the ability of reaching self-fulfillment, of having pride in what you can achieve, and of making your heart happy.

Wanting to make a difference, whether in the world or in your own heart, is all about having that fire.

Sounds wonderful, doesn't it?

Are you still looking for it, that thing that can become your fire?

Or, do you already have a desire, the start of a fire that resembles a match, but you're not quite sure what to do next?

Keep reading.

DIANA STOUT

CHAPTER 4: What is True Success?

Success isn't a one-size-fits-all. In fact, when asking writers about their successful journeys, it's amazing how every story is different. They're never the same, not even close.

Our fires aren't the same either, even though many of us have fires in the same arena, but every fire and each journey in discovery of that fire is unique.

For writers, success is about writing a book, selling it, and seeing our name in print.

One definition of success that has always stuck with me is: Success is preparedness meeting opportunity. While opportunities come and go all the time, if you're not ready, no opportunity is going to work. Building your fire is about preparedness.

Once you find your fire, you'll discover it's tied to your gut instinct, your determination, your desire to do well, your enthusiasm, all of which will be connected to a level of stick-to-itiveness that will be tested throughout that fire's lifetime and your participation with it.

Additionally, once you find your fire, you get to

determine what level of competence you want to achieve.

Looking back, my journey as an adult began in negativity. I was unhappy with my jobs—they were a means to an end, an income to pay bills, and it took a full-time job and several part-time jobs to pay those minimal bills. Women were not paid well and had no voice during those years. Additionally, I was unhappy that my path through life was limited and in the hands of others. I had no real autonomy. I was angry that adulthood was looking very much like childhood, where others controlled so much. I became the most unhappy, pessimistic, negative, whiny, complaining person you never wanted to meet.

Early on, as much as discovering my fire thrilled me, my inability to get published beyond a newspaper column and a few magazine articles frustrated me. I became jealous of others, those writers who appeared to have both that autonomy and success. I struggled to get my writing to another level.

The biggest conflict in that struggle was with myself. I'd become so mired in the swamps of my own negativity, I began losing friends.

I had become my own worst enemy.

As a result, I nearly fully extinguished my own fire, choking my inner core with that negativity.

My solution? I turned toward my fire. Writing became my friend, my focus. I poured myself into those words and started learning about positivity, embracing it and using it to change my thinking and outlook.

I started selling more articles and short stories.

Much later, after publishing my books, when I began teaching *Finding Your Fire* as a class, one of the first activities I assigned was to list what success meant to each student. These are the words and phrases they posted on the board:

- validation
- acceptance
- accepting both the good and the bad
- taking time for each other
- listening without judgement
- being generous of self
- seeing all that is good in ourselves and in others
- being connected to all humans
- coming together in respectful, honest, sincere ways that encourages, allows, promotes, and challenges us to be our best selves
- giving our best and doing our best
- unconditional caring and interest for the well-being and success of others
- caring deeply
- being irresistibly desired

- being happy

Are you seeing a common denominator here?

The list is about inner core values, which are attached to what we do. Do you notice how there aren't any physical attainments here, like accumulating lots of money, houses, vacations, and so forth?

For some people, success in work, family, and other activities are enough. Some people are satisfied without having a creative fire that is theirs alone. Their fire is, instead, centered around family activities and daily care. Overall, they have no desire to reach the pinnacle of self-actualization.

So, who are these people who want to reach that top level of self-actualization?

They're singers, artists, writers, people who build furniture, sew quilts, and perform a number of other creative crafts where they get to express or perform artistically. Some adopt children or are foster parents. Others save horses, dogs, whales, or clean beaches. They plant trees, build bird houses, plant flowers. They invent, lead, teach, recycle, reuse, and rescue. Whatever it is that they pursue, that pursuit fulfills them.

The bottom line is that they all want to make a difference in the world.

Those who are making a difference do it as if no one is watching. They would do it even if there was no money involved.

Some gain great attention, many do not.

Regardless of what they do, they pursue their passion with an open heart and a willingness of time and effort *because* they want to make a difference. If not only for themselves but for others, too.

You may look at some of these people and not see their success, but it doesn't matter what you think or can't see. It only matters what they think and how they feel.

Being successful isn't about who has the most toys, the most money, or the best title of the community, company, or country.

Being successful is what provides you with the feeling of self-fulfillment, of pride in what you're achieving and have achieved, and what makes your heart happy.

And, here's the real secret: you *can* make a difference—one person at a time. Groups and crowds aren't needed. Making a difference doesn't have to be huge or grand.

Take this book as an example. If I can make a difference with just one person, then I've been successful. However, if this book became wildly popular, then I'd have made even more of a difference.

Success Assignment

Before going forward and doing exercises and activities to determine your fire, what is your overall definition of success? What does being successful look like for you?

Write it down in a few sentences or paragraph. Describe what your life would be like.

Once you're written it down, put the description aside. We'll return to it later.

CHAPTER 5: What's Your *Why*?

Simon Sinek in his Ted Talk, "Start with *Why*," states that you want to know your *Why*, your purpose for getting out of bed each day.

Sinek goes on to say that earning an income isn't an answer. That's what you do to pay the bills. You might be getting out of bed every morning because the alarm goes off and you have to show up on time, but that's not the answer Sinek is looking for.

Earning an income is not what you do to find self-fulfillment, nor can it be called your *Why* here either, not unless you're one of the few fortunate people who is able to earn a living from your fire, from your passion that burns within.

So, what if there was no morning alarm? What if you didn't have children or a spouse—no one you were responsible for? No responsibilities whatsoever. What activity would you love to be doing every day?

Your *Why* is the fire, the passion that feeds your inner core, that gives you a self-satisfying purpose for living unlike a job that simply pays the bills.

Ideally, you'd like to tie your fire into work that becomes your career, which then becomes play. I was fortunate that I got to do that late in life as a writing professor, but not everyone can make it happen. And, now that I'm writing full time again, every day is playtime.

Simon Sinek states that Martin Luther King gave an "I Have a Dream" speech, not an "I Have a Plan" speech. We follow people because of their dreams.

Passion Assignment

So, if your passion comes from your inner core, what is the outer thing you want to do to manifest that passion? Something you can create or do that provides concrete evidence of that fire within?

What activity gets you fired up? That arouses your desire to spend endless hours doing it, where once you get into *the zone* that time flies? Where you may think you've only been working for an hour, but when looking at the clock, you realize you've been working for three hours instead?

Make a list of your passions.

My list would include everything related to nature and science—earth science and universal science, everything paranormal, everything medieval, and everything British history including everything royal. I'm passionate about puzzles, movies, books, pizza, and lasagna, European landscapes, and ancient cultures and civilizations.

What do these things have to do with my fire?

Everything and nothing. Within an interest can be that spark of an unrecognized fire. Patterns can reveal a fire, too.

What is your list looking like?

--

The story of finding my fire continues . . .

When in my 30s, I finally realized my *Why* was centered squarely in the writing field. Also, I wanted to share what I was learning, but I had little experience about life and no education to back up the writing. Even back then I wanted a Ph.D. but realized it was an impossible dream. As was my way at the time, I settled for less—shelving the education dream permanently. So I thought.

I turned wholeheartedly toward the writing and threw myself into the doing. I kept writing and submitting to publishers and entering contests.

While I was hoping for quick monetary success that would solve a myriad of day-to-day problems, such wasn't my path.

Not until I was almost 50, having had little enthusiasm for any job I'd ever worked, did I realize that I needed to turn my fire into my day job.

This was where I realized I could blow the cobwebs off that shelved education dream.

Four years later, after receiving my B.A. while working full time and going to school full time, I earned a scholarship to obtain my Master of Fine Arts (MFA) degree, which allowed me to teach writing at the four-year university level.

I was finally able to quit my day job.

Even though my creative writing time was replaced with academic writing, I was teaching about writing and loved it!

Work for a paycheck was no longer work; work had become play.

My students told me that I smiled when talking about writing. They said my passion for writing was catching. They in turn found a returned interest in English classes and were enjoying writing again.

They had observed and felt my *Why*. And, they followed me from class to class.

In the beginning, my writing *Why* was to earn money, to see my byline.

As I started publishing short articles and stories, getting favorable comments and encouragement from editors, readers, and other writers, my *Why* changed to include wanting to share, to inform readers.

And then, as I became more experienced and had a

solid education in writing, I added to my *Why*: I wanted to help other writers.

Today those are still my *Whys* for readers and other writers:

- wanting to share and entertain
- wanting to inform and educate
- wanting to help them grow their own writing skills

I know beyond a shadow of a doubt that I'm making a difference by the comments and follows I receive. By the stories students have told me how my class(es) changed their lives. By the number of downloads my dissertation has obtained since its publication, downloads from other countries that include education institutions, governments, businesses, organizations, and the military.

Whenever I'm writing, I feel at one with the universe.

My heart is happy.

Why Assignment

So, what is your *Why*? Write it down.

Don't be surprised if your *Why* changes over time. It's a sign of inner growth.

Think of your *Why* as your own mission statement.

It took a while for me to discover my true inner core,

to find my *Why*. Don't be discouraged if it takes you a while to really discover your inner core, too.

Once you do, no one will ever be able to deter you from it, unless you *allow* them to deter you.

CHAPTER 6: What's Your Passion Quotient?

That question isn't about romance passion. The question refers to the passion you have for your work. The fire in your heart. If you had to rate that passion level right now on a scale from 1-10, what would it be?

Mine rates a consistent 9-10 pretty much all the time now. It isn't unusual for me to have days where I'm at my desk all day long and into the night. I can do this because I'm retired and live alone in an apartment with no required outside upkeep (mowing, shoveling snow). My time is my own.

Granted, finding the time—let alone the passion—was a struggle when I was working outside the home and raising a family. Back then, my rating would have been more like an 8. Even so, I kept returning to that passion because it helped me cope with struggles I was having outside of my fire and in my life. The fire provided a focus and a reprieve from those struggles.

At one point, while in my 40s, my passion was high (at a 10) but little writing was getting done. I had three jobs where I was working 30 hours a week as a bank teller, another 15 as a bookkeeper for my husband's business, and I was a tutor liaison between two county libraries and a community college. Additionally, I had two teenagers at home. And then suddenly, based on my query and outline, I had a contract and an editorial deadline.

Despite everything else I was doing, I managed to spend 35 hours a week writing, and I was able to maintain that schedule for the duration of writing that book because of that high passion quotient rating.

Can you raise your passion quotient?

Most definitely. The exercise here can help you achieve that by getting you to analyze how you spend your time. Consider your *Why* as you do this assignment.

Passion Quotient Evaluation Assignment

- Think about your social life (real time and online), and consider the *Why* behind the activities you list. In participating, what is your take-away? What do you gain? How do you feel after each activity?

- What are different things you can do that will help you raise your passion quotient level?

- Could you put less energy into other activities,

reserving some of that energy for your fire?

Has your passion quotient number risen a point or two after reading this chapter?

Ideally, you want your fire to give you purpose, but at the same time, you don't want that fire to become injurious to your job or family. It's about finding a balance.

As we've done with the other assignments, once you're finished, save it, and set it aside. We'll come back to your notes here later.

DIANA STOUT

Part II: Universal Laws

"If you want to find the secrets of the universe, think in terms of energy, frequency and vibration."

- Nikola Tesla

DIANA STOUT

CHAPTER 7: Important Universal Laws

Growing up, I'd never heard about the Universal Laws. What a difference my life and my attitude would have been had I known about these laws as a child or even as a teenager.

My research revealed that there doesn't appear to be an exact number of these laws. Some say there are seven, others say twelve, or more.

The ones I'm including here are the ones that I've used, followed, and observed, always with amazing results. Their principles and philosophies are near and dear to my heart.

The Law and Principle of Time

Interestingly enough, there is both a Law of Time and a Principal of Time.

The Law of Time refers to the universal *natural timing* that factors synchronization of the universe, determined via mathematics in the universe's creation. Even though this law became a major rabbit hole where I spent enjoyable time learning about it, this law has little to do with our fires.

The Principle of Time—totally different from the Law of Time—features the *artificial timing* created by man in the form of calendars and clocks. This principle has everything to do with our fires.

Would you be surprised to learn that the Principle of Time favors no one person or thing?

Everyone and everything on this planet receives the same 168 hours per week with no discrimination of age, sex, gender identity, race, political affiliation, religion, health, wealth, or beliefs.

The only disparity that exists is between those who've learned how to manage *their* time and those who struggle to find time.

Law of Polarity

Everything has an opposite in its element.

- Yin, Yang
- Strong, Weak
- Love (or Hate), Indifference
- Action, Reaction
- Light, Dark
- Happy, Sad
- Fast, Slow
- Success, Failure

And, so forth.

The thing is, you can't fully appreciate one side

without having experienced the other.

Law of Abundance

Also known as the Law of Compensation. This law is all about reaping what you sow, about being rewarded for work achieved, not just for a paycheck but for compensation of emotion for doing your best and about performing good deeds and paying it forward.

A fundamental principle of this Law is that whatever you need is already yours, available to you when needed, providing you understand how the flow of abundance works.

When we focus on our lacks, we shut down that flow.

The Law of Abundance is tied to the Law of Attraction, which is detailed further in this chapter.

The Law of Abundance isn't about riches of money, grandiose homes, fancy cars. The Law of Abundance is about your vibration being in sync with universal vibrations so that the flow of abundance can flow toward you.

So, where is your focus? You have to choose. Will you focus on your lack or on your abundance, which includes your gratitude?

Once upon a time, my focus was on what I lacked. I stayed in that lacking state of mind until I finally chose to focus on abundance and feeling that I had everything I needed. Only then did my circumstances change. Now, I'll choose abundance every time.

Law of Action

The Law of Action is about *action* (motion) and *reaction*. Every action has a reaction. There is not one action that doesn't have a reaction somewhere as either positive or negative.

A writing example:

Action – You give your manuscript to a beta reader. It's returned with a lot of comments and corrections.

#1 Reaction – You think and believe: I'm a lousy writer. I'm no good. I'm never going to sell anything. That reader is just jealous of me and is out to make me look bad. I'll never use her again.

#2 Reaction – You think and believe: Oh, wow, there're more mistakes here than I knew. I need to proof my work better. Maybe I need to hire an editor before I use beta readers.

Which scenario best describes your initial reactionary style to events and people: #1 or #2?

So, what does the Law of Action have to do with your fire?

Everything.

The Law of Action is important because it's all about how *you* react, which then affects other Laws as you'll soon see.

Law of Attraction

The Law of Attraction embraces what you think, what you say, meaning the things you think about and talk about are the very things you attract toward you.

Are you now considering what your last thoughts have been about? Trying to remember what you've said lately? And, to whom?

This law has become one of my favorites because I've seen it in action many times.

The Law of Attraction is powerful because *you* rule the Law. And, you've been ruling it without even realizing it. With your thoughts. With your words.

There was a time when I was saying, "I'm so sick and tired of [fill in the blank]." I said it a lot; I said it about everything. Every single day.

Guess what?

I started becoming physically tired and sick. Really sick. Lots of colds, walking pneumonia, headaches, and tired beyond belief.

I had attracted being sick and tired via my words.

Not until I started listening to Norman Vincent Peale and Anthony Robbins, who stressed in their books and tapes that we create our lives, did I realize what I was doing.

This Law fully embraces the Law of Action—in how *you* act and in how *you* react.

Doubtful in the beginning, my first conscious attempt of testing the Law of Attraction was with a non-writing issue.

The kids were young, money was tight, and I needed a winter coat. What I could afford was about $20 less than what coats were selling for. In my mind's eye, I saw the coat: long, plaid in browns and with a hood. Whenever I was in a store, I looked for it.

Then one day, I found an inexpensive pumpkin-colored winter hat on sale. I knew it would be a perfect match with my desired coat. I bought the hat, knowing the coat was on its way toward me.

Three weeks later, I found and bought the coat. It was exactly as I had pictured it and the color of the hat was one of the colors in the coat, which was a long, brown and pumpkin plaid, cotton coat that buttoned and tied at the waist, with a hood.

I wore that coat for a decade and it was wonderfully warm against the harsh winters we received that decade. Winters that included blizzards and the coldest temperatures we'd ever had up until that time.

I had attracted that coat via my thoughts.

Once realization of this power occurs, that's when you want to start consciously testing your ability to harness the Law, or any of the Laws, for that matter.

With my half dozen small tests where each became more important, they all proved that my subconscious—I call it my little voice—was always right. I learned I could trust it 100%.

That little voice has never failed me. Ever. Not even in giant decisions, where practical reasoning *appeared* to be the best choice. The subconscious knows!

Here's the thing—your subconscious cannot tell what is real or unreal, but it listens well. It listens to what you say, what you think, and it believes *everything*, whether or not it's the truth or whether it's positive or negative.

Have you ever been thinking of someone only to get a phone call, email, or text from them that same day? Law of Attraction at work.

Have you ever thought about an object that you wanted to shop for and suddenly all kinds of ads—on TV, on the internet, in the mail—start showing up? Law of Attraction at work.

These are actual situations. But, how about the unreal?

Have you ever had a dream where you were being chased or in a horrific situation that frightened you? Did you wake up in a sweat, your heart racing?

Your body didn't know it was a dream and yet your subconscious was reacting to what the brain received in that dream as if the event were real. Again, the Law of Attraction at work.

Whatever the mind imagines, it is felt by the body *and* is attracted to you. Always. It doesn't matter if what you imagine is negative or positive. Either way, the subconscious listens and delivers.

We are what we think.

We are what we say.

We are what we do, which includes how we react.

Pay attention to your words.

Pay attention to your thoughts.

Pay attention to your actions *and* your reactions.

Law of Vibration

People and things of similar vibrations are attracted to each other. This statement explains how the Law of

Attraction works.

This law is why you want to always be thinking about the thing(s) you desire and not about past events that trigger your anger and keep you stuck in the past.

Anytime you find your thoughts in the past, purposefully focus on your future, what you want coming toward you instead.

The Law of Vibration is why you want to let go of your anger, your frustrations, and rise above feelings of sadness and disappointment. While it's human nature to feel sad about any loss and to feel disappointment that you didn't win a contest or get the job, it's not okay to stay focused within those feelings because when you do, you create vibrations other energies will pick up on, attracting repeats of those disappointments.

Wouldn't you rather have your vibrations attract like-minded people and situations toward your fire rather than the alternative of continuing to live in worry and anxiety?

Did you know that your energy always arrives before you do? And, that your vibrations get sent out with your thoughts? Believe it or not, those vibrations can travel long distances.

Want to test it? Send out a thought that you want [insert name] to contact you. See how long it takes before it happens. Don't be surprised if they say, "I was just thinking about you." It means they picked up on the vibration you sent them.

Change your thoughts and your vibration will change. Change your vibration and everything around you changes.

You may be saying, *no one can change their thoughts*.

Yes, you can.

Whenever I find myself going down a not-so-good path of worry, anxiety, or stress about a situation over which I have little to no control, I intentionally turn my focus elsewhere, usually on to a writing project even if I do nothing more than cleaning files or some needed editing.

As I change my thinking, I give up all those worries to the Universe, asking it to handle the situation. It always does.

You, too, can control your thoughts, thus controlling the vibrations you send out.

Law of Karma

This is the Universal Law that most people refer to and know. Are you noticing how similar these Laws are to one another?

With the Law of Karma, what you send out comes back to you tenfold. This Law is also known as the Law of Cause and Effect.

For the good of your own energy, your vibration, and your fire, this is the Law where you want to forgive others who have harmed you, whether they know it or not. And, if their negativity continues to be toxic, you want to remove yourself from their proximity, if you can. At the very least, create some distance by protecting your vibration.

Forgiving isn't about letting them off the hook. Forgiveness is about dealing with your emotions, your thoughts.

It's about *letting go* of ill-will, anger, revenge, anything negative. Forgiveness is about letting go and handing whatever the issue is over to the Universe to take care of the offender(s).

Many times, I've seen Karma do Her work quickly. Other times, it's taken months, if not years. It's up to Her when She'll do the work—all in Her time, not yours. Never yours.

Whenever I'm about to enter into a known conflict of any kind, even with weather, I pull down a protective veil around me that acts like a protective barrier, even a mirror sometimes. It works!

Just know that negative thoughts become negative feelings, and all that negativity will keep your vibrational energy low. Negative vibrations can kill your fire and all the good you've done with the Law of Attraction and other Laws.

Letting go requires practice. The more I do it, the easier it becomes. Letting go has become such a habit that I now repeat this phrase often during trying times:

*How others treat me is their Karma. How I react is **my** Karma.*

Universal Laws Conclusion

You get to decide what your response will be. Always.

Do you react without thinking? You can change that. Instead, choose to think first, react second.

The question is, do you want to be in control of your thoughts? Your reactions?

In summary, these Laws are exacting. There's no wiggle room. No grey area.

I had to work really hard to change my thinking, the basis of operation for these Laws. It was hard, especially when situations felt stuck and unmoving.

It's easy to be negative, way harder to be positive and mean it.

Either you follow these Laws and they work for you—in their time—or you continue as you've been doing, wondering why nothing works out the way you want, where you continue to worry and continue to deal with unrelenting anxiety and stress.

If you really want these Laws to work for you, you have to do the work, which will put you on the path of operation from the side of positivity.

No one has power over your emotions except you. Over time, you'll stop reacting to the negativity and will discover you have more energy for your fire.

The main thing I've noticed about these Laws and the lessons they bring with them is that if you don't learn the lesson, you're doomed to repeat it with a different person, in a different landscape, a different situation, at a later time. Despite the differences, the overarching lesson will be the same.

As you learn the lessons, you'll rise higher on the ladder of peace and wisdom, wanting to devote more time to your fire.

Eventually, you'll find your place of prosperity that works well for you and will be able to ignore the naysayers or those who are trying to sway you away from your fire.

You'll recognize that what works for you probably won't work for anyone else.

You'll begin to notice that it's okay to be different.

And finally, you'll realize that it's not your

responsibility to make others happy or for them to make you happy. That each one of you has to create your own happiness, that your happiness derives from your fire, your inner core.

We are the owners of what we create, including our thoughts and our vibrations.

Part III: Finding Your Fire

"Pay attention to the things you are naturally drawn to. They are often connected to your path, passion, and purpose in life."

– Ruben Chavez

CHAPTER 8: Discovering Your Fire

So, now, we come to the heart of this book: you either want to know how to find your fire, or you want to know how to keep it hot.

Exercises I've done and have shared with my students on how to find your fire, I now share with you. The exercises work.

This chapter is about discovery and the best way to start—you guessed it(!)—is to make a pencil-and-paper list.

The problem with keeping a brainstorming list in your head is that you are creating a dam, not allowing the flow of ideas to occur. Generally, the list in your head contains only about seven items. You want to uncover *everything*.

There's magic in writing things down, in using paper and pencil. Call it another universal law or principle. Neuroscience has uncovered that when we write down our goals, we have a better chance of achieving them.

Recording my thoughts opens a floodgate of ideas, which is what true brainstorming is about. Do you really want to cheat yourself out of that experience, that success?

I challenge you to skip the electronic list and use paper and pencil.

Discovery Assignment

Write down your hobbies or even interests in hobbies you're not doing currently. Include those you've done in the past, those you're considering doing in the future.

This list will differ from your list of passions because this list is about actions, things you do or create with your hands. If there are duplicates on both lists, that's okay. Don't overthink it. Let the duplication occur.

Write the list fast, then walk away from it and return to it as needed until you feel there's nothing more to add.

Don't delete anything! While you can cross something off, don't delete, remove, or erase anything while creating this list.

It's important not to delete anything while creating because deleting stops the creative process and moves you into the editing process. Editing will occur in the next step. Don't get ahead of yourself.

Continue creating your list until it feels finished.

Editing the List

Now, under each activity, add a few details, any criteria that helps you in considering the activity, like supplies needed, outside resources you might want to use, cost factors, your enjoyment factor, anything that crosses your mind as you write this activity down.

Estimate how much time you spend on this activity over a day, week, or month's time. There is no right or wrong answer here. If you don't know exactly, guess.

Consider detailing the pros and cons of each item.

I began noticing that many of my passions were sole activities—which suited me just fine since I wanted my fire to not involve anyone else.

Additionally, expenses were a factor for me, along with transportation. I made note of these cons.

Again, use a criterion that fits your needs.

Looking Ahead

As you analyze this list, where do you see yourself with each activity a year from now?

Five years from now?

Can you see yourself building a career out of this activity? Do you want to? This was the question that really had me separating casual hobbies—things that kept my hands busy—from possible fires.

The thing is, you're not making any final decisions yet. You're only speculating here.

Examine your energy while creating this list. Make note if an activity has you reacting. Are you feeling positive or negative? Don't analyze the feelings. Just acknowledge and record them.

Does any activity generate more interest than others?

Can you feel your passion growing?

The more I looked at this list, the more I realized writing had been my dream but one I had discounted because I didn't think it possible to achieve.

Go ahead, consider the dream achievable! By writing it down, you're planting the seed. Should you choose that dream, you're deciding to nurture, expand, and live that dream.

You can make that dream your reality!

CHAPTER 9: Making a Decision

Now that you've created your list and have added detailed notes, take a look at it.

At first glance, what do you notice? Are there mostly outdoor activities or indoor? Quiet versus loud? Activities requiring supplies or none at all? Do you see any patterns?

There was a time when I had lots of passions, lots of hobbies, lots of interests.

Many of us are multi-potentialities, people with multiple interests in multiple fields. It's not a bad thing having different interests.

With all my interests, I felt pulled in different directions. The things I really wanted to do and finish weren't getting done. The ones I finished, like the needlepoint, felt decorative with no special meaning. I began questioning my purpose.

Once I listed all of my interests, I asked myself: If I could follow only one of these pursuits for the rest of my life, devoting my time only to it, which one would it be?

For me, writing kept floating up to the top, but was it really my fire?

Whittling Down the List

Not sure which item is your fire, yet?

I didn't know for sure when first looking at my list. So, I began comparing one item to another, choosing which would I rather do if I had to make a choice and eliminate one over the other. Like this:

- cross-stitch vs painting – I chose needlepoint
- needlepoint vs quilting – I chose needlepoint
- needlepoint vs writing – I chose writing

And, so forth. Compare any and all activities you believe could be your fire.

I was surprised to discover writing took precedence over everything else. I wouldn't have thought that because I spent more time on everything else instead.

But, there was a certain joy I received when writing that I didn't get from the other activities. That's why writing climbed to the top of my list.

From this exercise, my downtime from writing became watching movies or reading—both of which fed into my writing—and putting jigsaw puzzles together. The puzzles provide me time to think about my writing, especially when I was stuck and needed time to reflect.

As much as I enjoyed painting, I didn't get the same joy from it as I did from writing. For a while, I kept the needlework supplies, but eventually, I got rid of it and all the painting supplies. I wasn't participating enough to justify the space the supplies required.

Once I got rid of all remnants of these activities, I was surprised there wasn't any twinge of disappointment that I was giving them up. The activities had served their purpose at the time, but now they were taking time away from the one thing I was becoming most passionate about—where my true fire resided.

Comparing and choosing is a great exercise for decluttering and downsizing, too. I've done it with books, wall hangings, pictures, clothing, dishes, furniture, and so forth.

In trying to determine your fire, ask yourself the question I did once I discovered my #1 choice:

> *If you could only do this one activity for the rest of your life, can you see yourself doing it year after year?*

I could. Even though I didn't know where that future would lead me, I could see myself writing for the rest of my life. In fact, in choosing to write, a whole new world opened up to me.

As you look at your #1 choice, can you feel the fire intensify?

Are you as surprised by your #1 choice as I was? Or, is it a flame that you already had but now want to make even hotter?

Part IV: Now What?

"If you don't know where you're going, any road will take you there."

    – Cheshire Cat, *Alice in Wonderland*
        by Lewis Carroll

The water doesn't flow until the faucet is turned on.

        - Louis L'Amour

DIANA STOUT

CHAPTER 10: Making a Plan

Once you've made your decision, keep brainstorming on paper. What does your fire's future look like? What are the different ways to approach your fire?

There is no right or wrong place to start.

Keep It Secret

For the time being, keep your plan to yourself, unless it's with a like-minded tribe. As much as you're going to want to share your new plan, don't do it.

When I began to write, I didn't tell anyone other than my best friend at the time what I was doing. She was extremely supportive. In fact, it was one of her comments that spurred me into what would be my start as a weekly newspaper columnist.

After the first column came out, friends and family were surprised I hadn't said anything. A case where showing was more effective than telling.

My mistake came a few years later, when I announced to friends and family I was going to write a book.

Most of them laughed or ridiculed, reminding me that I had no real experience or education. Just because I was writing a column, what did I know about writing a book?

Fortunately, I was able to dismiss their comments. Since I was used to submissions being rejected, I didn't take the comments personally; but in short order, I had discovered who I could trust and who I couldn't. Who was supportive and who wasn't.

The other reason you don't want to talk too much about your plans is that in the telling, you end up giving away a lot of your power.

Not sure you believe it? Create an experiment by taking two similar ideas of a plan or a purchase you've been thinking about, something you've not been able to decide so far. Write down your own thoughts about each one, both the pro and the con.

Now, go and tell people about one but not the other.

Make note of their advice. Is their advice geared toward your interests or their own? Do they focus on the negatives (con) or the positives (pro)?

Did their input diminish your excitement?

As a result of their opinion, which one are you still excited about?

The same thing happens with your fire.

CHAPTER 11: Setting Goals

Setting goals is important to getting your fire started and then keeping it hot.

The problem is, as we get started, we tend to create goals that are too large, and then we become frustrated when we're unable to meet them.

Go ahead and set big goals. There's nothing wrong with dreaming big. It's only by dreaming big that we can accomplish that goal.

Then, break your goal down into chunks. And then, break the chunks down into the smallest task possible.

Being able to cross off several small tasks from your to-do list will feel like you've accomplished a lot.

Recognize that every week could be different regarding the amount of time you spend with your fire's goal and learn to celebrate those differences, rolling with the changes.

Know that performing any writing task is about experiencing the journey of that fire.

While achieving success with the end product is nice,

life is really about the journey of the fire.

The only guarantee I can make, based on my own experience, is that the more time you spend with your fire, the more enjoyable it becomes.

CHAPTER 12: Building Your Fire Properly

In the beginning of any new venture, our enthusiasm burns hot. The problem is, we burn out quickly.

Then, we find ourselves not understanding why it's a struggle to find that enthusiasm again. We start questioning our ability, even our desire in having this dream.

The real problem is that we didn't build our fire properly.

Out in the wilderness when building a physical fire, we begin with fire-starting material called *tinder*, which can be wood shavings, moss, dry leaves, tiny dry sticks—all small combustible items that flame up and burn quickly

Once that's lit, then we add *kindling*—small pieces of dry wood.

Once enough kindling has burned, providing decent continuing flames where the *main fuel* can burn, that's when we add bigger pieces of wood—branches—until we're finally able to burn logs that keeps the fire going, and which when enough logs have burned adds coals to the base of the fire.

In the beginning, I was throwing logs onto a fire that had grown cold, expecting them to burn.

Rather than spending ten minutes every day, which could have created momentum, I was waiting for those 2-3 hour time periods where I thought I would get lots more writing done.

The exact opposite turned out to be true! Those big chunks of time were few and far between, and I achieved little during that time because I spent so much effort in revisiting what I'd already done.

I learned I needed to pace myself and use spare minutes here and there (my tinder) rather than expecting to find three hours each weekend (main fuel) that I'd have free.

I learned I could write while on a playground or in an airport. I could edit a page while at a stoplight. I could dictate new words, especially dialogue, into a recorder while driving.

When my kids were little, I learned to write when they napped. At night after they went to bed, I found myself too tired mentally to write, but I was able to perform mindless chores that didn't require much thought.

--

In building your fire, identify your tinder, the fire starters. Those small tasks that you can do easily.

Identify your kindling, the small sticks that can catch the flame easily and start burning. Those tasks that require just a little bit more effort and that can get your fire going again.

Then, finally identify your main fuel. These are the big goals you want to achieve, the ones you want to break into fire starters and then kindling tasks to get your fire flaming.

Build your fire properly and you'll stay excited, wanting to return to your fire day after day, week after week. Before long, you'll find your big goals—the branches and logs—have caught fire and are burning. And even better—you'll still feel energized when you have to walk away from your writing for a short time.

I've learned if I skipped too many days of not writing, my fire starts cooling. Sometimes to get started again, I'll clean out writing files, clean off my desk, perform some research, or any other writing chore that gets me back into the mindset of writing again. These are my tinder, my fire starters.

Also, I've learned that by using a paper planner at night, I can plan what I want to achieve the next day, which preps me ahead of time and alerts my subconscious. (See the next chapter.)

In summary, to build your fire properly, start small. And, spend time regularly with your fire so that it won't burn out.

CHAPTER 13: Helping Your Subconscious

Remember how I told you the subconscious can't tell the difference between what's real or unreal?

Well, the subconscious also has the power to manifest the unreal into real.

This powerful ability of our subconscious is why you don't want to berate yourself negatively in thought or speech. You want your self-talk to be positive and encouraging.

Because I have such a natural inclination to say, *You dummy, why did you do that?* I've learned to discipline myself by saying, *Considering the situation, you did fine. You'll do better next time.*

A way for me to feed my subconscious with positivity is to surround myself with other writers. In the beginning, even though I only got to meet with them once a month, at the expense of an entire day and babysitting money, that meeting was worth attending, because I came home inspired and energized. For me, those meetings acted like kindling.

Now, with today's online forums and meeting platforms such as Zoom and Messenger, I get to connect with writers every day. As a result, I want to write more and I do.

At the beginning of my writing career, I learned to use self-talk positivity and say aloud, *I am a good writer.* It didn't matter what the reality was. My subconscious need to hear that I *was* a good writer.

Over time, I became a better writer. In fact, I had editors and publishers telling me they loved my voice. Even though they'd just rejected a manuscript, they wanted me to keep submitting.

Recently, I rediscovered an email from a Hollywood production company from a couple years ago, that said, "She's a writer to watch."

These are comments I keep in the forefront as reminders because they feed my fire.

Other Things To Do To Help Your Subconscious

Write and post affirmations where you'll see them frequently. I used to tape mine to the bathroom mirror. I've posted them next to my computer, on the wall across the room using huge Post-Its, and on regular Post-It notes in my planner, moving them from week to week.

Visualize your end product. See yourself accepting writing awards, helping others, whatever is your fire's purpose. See yourself as successful.

When I had decided I was going to write a book, for inspired visualization, I took a book, wrapped it with clean paper, wrote my title and name on the front with a stick-figure drawing and propped it next to my computer. I saw my name on that cover every day as I wrote my first book.

Listen to mood music. I've learned that I can change my mood by listening to specific music — soundtracks of different genres for instance, or Baroque music, also known as brain music to writers and teachers.

Plan your next day just before going to bed. Why? Because our subconscious tends to work on those things we last think about. If you're struggling to resolve an issue, think about it just before falling asleep. Write down your plan writing-wise for the next day and see if you don't wake up energized and can hardly wait to get to your desk.

I often use this exercise when I'm struggling with a plot or a character, asking that I be given a way to fix it all when I wake up. It works! Try it.

Remember This

- You are what you think.
- You are what you say.
- You are what you visualize.
- You are what you believe.
- Believe in you.
- Believe in your fire.

DIANA STOUT

Part V: When the Fire Dies

"One reason people resist change is because they focus on what they have to give up, instead of what they have to gain."

— Rick Godwin

"The secret of change is to focus all of your energy, not on fighting the old, but on building the new."

— Socrates

DIANA STOUT

CHAPTER 14: How Fires Die

Our creative fires are more fragile than we know. We make that discovery when it is dying or already dead.

Here are a few ways a writer's fire can die:

- Worry, Anxiety, & Stress
- Criticism
- Reviews
- Life Events
- Overextended or Overcommitted
- Daily Sacrifices

Worry, Anxiety, & Stress

Life is filled with stress.

Events we didn't create can impact us: weather related disasters, fires, loss of jobs, accidents, and so forth.

People impact us as well: co-workers, family, friends, classmates, shoppers, and people around us when we're in a crowd.

Stress can create anxiety, and then we're having to

learn how to live with that anxiety so it doesn't mess with our mental or physical well-being.

Because of our anxiety, we start to worry.

- Will my child be safe if I let them (fill in the blank)?
- Is it safe to be on the road when (fill in the blank)?
- Should I stay with this job if it's making me feel (fill in the blank)?

Far too often we can't control these events that other entities—people, animals, and weather—produce, but we can control how we react.

Remember the Law of Action? The things we can't control is the *action* part of the law. How we respond is the *reaction*.

Did you know that we often create our own anxiety because we start worrying about something of which we have no control?

Stress is a *reaction*.

Anxiety is a *reaction*.

Worry is a *reaction* based on previous actions or your own imaginary *what if*s.

The goal is to learn how to control your reaction(s). Learning how not to react is a practiced skill that can be learned.

It's about staying calm and cool. Analyzing while observing. Thinking before speaking. Not reacting emotionally. Concentrating on the facts only, not letting someone's emotional reaction of trying to segue us away from the facts.

Have you ever said, *That he/she/them made me mad!*? Actually, the truth is you *allowed* them to make you mad. You handed over your power (the control of your emotion) to them.

Every attorney I've ever worked with has told me, "They're trying to get you to react so they can use it against you. Don't react. Don't respond."

I've learned that sometimes to get an issue out of my system, I respond via writing—journaling about the event, my feelings, what was said, what I wanted to say and didn't. And then just before tearing it all up, I ask the Universe to handle the situation, to bring clarity and change. Sometimes, I have to let it go several times to the Universe before I can finally forget about it.

When you discover you're feeling anxious or stressed about something, change your thinking by focusing on something else. If you're worrying, play that worry out. Consider, what's the worst that can happen? What's the best that can happen? Now that you've thought it through, let it go.

The goal in changing your focus is to put emotional distance between that stressful event or person and your thoughts. Writing it out allows the stress to flow out of you and onto paper. Take heed: never send it out! Destroy it, instead.

Worry, Anxiety, Stress Assignment

List what you worry about typically.

List what makes you anxious.

List what makes you feel stressful.

Can you see how suggestions of change could eliminate some of these items on your lists? Write the suggestions down. If you can't change any of the items, is there any way to lessen the impact they have on you?

If you're not happy with your past reactions, then consider how you can change your reactions in the future.

Criticism

For new writers, criticism that comes from those first critiques is like pouring a bucket of water on their fire.

The disappointment is deflating. First thoughts are: *I'm lousy. I can't write. What am I doing?*

The thing is, critiques aren't personal. Critiques are

about the words on the paper. It's the only thing a reader sees.

We have to teach ourselves that not everything said or done is personal to us.

More often than not, what is being said or done is a reflection or is personal to the critiquer. It's wise to remember the Law of Karma and the Law of Action here.

No words have power until you give those words power.

Always consider the source when receiving criticism:

- Are they a master in the field of that criticism?
- Are they also offering a way to fix the errors?
- Are they highly-rated by others?

If the answer to these questions is yes, then be glad they're helping you and celebrate the assistance.

If the answer to these questions is no, take the criticism with a grain of salt. Even so, is their intent to help? If so, there's nothing to begrudge.

Proper protocol from you as the recipient of criticism if you requested it from a beta reader, judge, and so forth, is to never defend. Just say *Thank you*. You can add, something like, *I'll take your suggestions into consideration*. Or, *You've provided some good ideas*.

After thinking about their advice for a few days, you

may be surprised to find that their criticism was spot-on and that you've now found a new beta reader.

Reviews

As a writer, the best advice you can receive about reviews is don't read them.

If you do choose to read the reviews so you can get quotes from the better ones, ignore the rest. Just let them go.

Don't respond to reviews. Everyone is allowed an opinion about your writing when you make it public, the same way you're allowed to post a review—your opinion—after you've read a book.

Reviews are nothing more than opinions. Granted, some opinions carry more weight than others because they come from experts of the field, but how many times have you disagreed with even those reviews? I have, lots of times.

Life Events

Anytime I was dealing with stressful events, which included deaths in the family, losing jobs, moving, and so forth, I would turn to my fire. My writing.

Writing was and still is my release, my safe place. I'm always able to pour out my feelings through the keystrokes. Much of that writing I'll tear up, but the thing is, I have a positive release valve.

Your fire should be your safe place, too. A place where you can restore yourself, find yourself again, and where it protects you against the onslaught of daily and weekly negatives that are just part of life.

Life events can include weather, accidents, deaths, births, marriages, illness, caring for others, moving, or other events that can create a seismic shift in your life.

Big life events bring big changes. Some changes are short-term, others long-term.

My own creative writing got sidelined for fifteen years when I returned to school for economic reasons and was writing academic papers instead. Thankfully, I was still writing, and in the long run, all that writing made me a better creative writer once I returned to it.

Overextended or Overcommitted

Our fire can easily dim or die when taking part in too many organizations, events, and other extra-curriculum activities.

If wondering whether you should continue with any of these activities, consider or ask yourself:

- Do you receive the same joy from belonging or performing as you once did?
- Do you feel drained or energized afterward?
- Do you prepare for the activity with a sense of dread?

Your answers will tell you if you should continue with the activity or not.

Daily Sacrifices

If you want your fire to heat up, then make it a priority on your list of things to do each day. Be prepared to make some sacrifices elsewhere.

My sacrifices included less socializing both in person with friends and online in social media, watching less TV, and reading fewer recreational books.

Writing energizes me. Watching TV calms me, which I do *after* I'm done writing for the day, allowing my brain, my writing thoughts to wind down.

We all have different priorities and different needs, whether seasonal or day-to-day. It's all about finding your rhythm while still tending to your fire.

--

In Summary

Think of yourself as a bank of energy, where deposits and withdrawals are made and recorded in the register.

Withdrawals are the negatives, as discussed in this chapter, that over time can dampen and extinguish your fire.

Deposits are the positives that help your fire burn

brighter.

What does your personal register look like? Are there more withdrawals than deposits? Is it any wonder you have no energy to work on your fire?

If there are more withdrawals from your energy bank than there are deposits, your account will surely become depleted and your fire will die.

DIANA STOUT

CHAPTER 15: Writer's Block

I don't believe in writer's block. I used to, but not anymore. I recognize it for what it really is—being stuck.

How did I come to that conclusion?

When I first started writing books, I would write them from beginning to end. One day, I sat staring at a computer screen for ten hours, unable to write one word. I believed I was experiencing writer's block.

I felt my fire dying. By the end of that day, I vowed I would never have that kind of experience ever again.

The next day, I decided to skip past that problematic scene in the book and start where I knew what was happening in the story. By the time I got to the end of the book, I knew what had to occur in that hole I had skipped.

Clearly, I had been able to write beyond that spot, so it couldn't be writer's block.

The same can be said for any fire. There will come a point where you will feel stuck.

Feel the fear, put a name to it, make notes there about

what you'd like to do there and then move past it. Do something different or work on it in a different way. Finish the project with the hole. You'll know what the hole needs by the time you finish that project's first draft.

The same thing occurs when we're learning or trying something new. That stuck place is called a learning plateau. You can only learn so much before you stall for a time.

I learned this while taking an algebra class. When stuck with a problem, I went and did something completely different, like playing the piano. Twenty minutes later, I could return to the math and continue without the earlier struggle.

I do the same thing with writing now. When I reach a stuck stage, I get up and go clean something, fold the laundry, run an errand.

When I return, I'm usually no longer stuck. If I return and find I'm still stuck, however, that's when I'll skip that area and move forward.

It's always about finding that passion again and following where the fire leads.

Part VI: Restarting Your Fire

"I would rather die of passion than of boredom."

– Vincent Van Gogh

"When you find yourself riding a dead horse, dismount."

– a Lakota saying

DIANA STOUT

CHAPTER 16: Making Changes

While living on the farm, whenever I went into the milking parlor as the cows were let in, I watched how they'd go into different stanchions[2], following each other as if in a line. And then, all of a sudden, one would stop and just stare at a cow in a certain stanchion even though there were several next to it that were empty.

I learned the cows had favorite stanchions and it would be a new cow that had just freshened (had a calf) who had taken another cow's spot.

Milking cows don't like change any more than we humans do.

Over the years, having divorced twice, having moved countless times—which means changing services and professionals—and having changed careers as well, I've learned that change is actually a good thing.

---

[2] A stanchions are stalls, side by side down the length of a barn, divided by minimal rails, where the animal inserts their head through a device that when closed holds them in place. Cows being milked eat grain while they're "held" in place. When the milking is finished, they're released.

Change means you get to reinvent yourself.

Change means you can start over.

Change provides an opportunity for new friends.

And, change can be small or big.

One of most beneficial changes for me occurred when I went from being the most negative person who wallowed in the past—someone you never wanted to meet—to one of positivity and living for the future.

I've been able to reinvent myself several times in big ways, countless times in smaller ways.

Change as a writer meant I became an indie publisher from a traditionally published author as I'd been in the past.

Having learned some of the various Universal Laws, which ones do you see as game changers for yourself?

Which Laws do you want to start using consciously?

What other changes do you want to make?

I've learned to let go of the past—of belongings, memories, pictures—anything that drags me away from my fire.

I want my focus squarely and securely on the future.

Change is good. Change is desirable.

Change your focus and you'll be changing that which you draw to yourself. The Law of Abundance, Law of Vibration, Law of Attraction, and Karma all are heavily affected by changes.

Sometimes changing your focus toward your fire in small ways can help make the fire burn even hotter than before.

Examples of Specific Changes You Can Make

Instead of blaming or making excuses, say, "I recognize I made a choice to [insert the activity] instead of writing today."

Instead of blaming an editor for rejecting your story, recognize that your story didn't fit what she was looking for. Or that it's possible your story needs more work.

Instead of criticizing and judging others, acknowledge your differences and wish them well with much success, and then put them out of your mind. Focus on something else instead.

Instead of berating yourself because of another rejection, instead congratulate yourself. A rejection means you made a submission, and took a step forward. Take more steps. Celebrate the rejections—it's a sign that you're writing more, tending to your fire.

Instead of making excuses for not facing your fears,

stop, and consider what's going on internally. Blogger Leesha Chamberlain states that our excuses come from our internal fears, which can be fear of failure, change, uncertainty, making mistakes, and lacking confidence.[3] Acknowledge your fears by facing them. It's the only way you break through those excuses and eliminate their triggers that create your fear, anxiety, or stress.

Instead of worrying—a useless activity that produces nothing worthwhile—hand the worrisome issue over to the Universe and ask it to take care of the situation and any people involved. It will. Then, focus on something else.

Stop Asking Everyone, "What Should I Do?"

Can asking for advice be a negative?

Yes.

When unsure of yourself, when afraid of making a mistake, that's when you'll ask others *what should I do?* You're looking for approval. You're looking for someone else to decide for you. That way if you fail, you can blame them having followed their advice.

The problem is, this is *your* fire, not theirs.

Your fire is within you, not always something that

---

[3] "The Reason We Make Excuses." May 24, 2019. From: https://wisdom-trek.com/the-reason-we-make-excuses/

anyone close to you can see.

You'll *know* you've found your fire and what's right for it because you'll get goosebumps or have an overwhelming sense of calm settle upon you.

When you find your fire, you'll know it. There won't be any doubts. You'll have this wonderful sense of knowing what this life has intended for you.

Raise Your Vibration

You control your vibrational energy. You. Only you.

Look for the lesson in all things . . . especially those things that give you anxiety, stress, and worry. Whatever it is that creates these troublesome three, let them go. Give the people and the situations up to the Universe for handling. Stop trying to resolve everything yourself.

Some examples of how I've let go and sought out assistance from the Universe recently:

- Universe, please help [insert name] to find what they need to help them out of their current problem(s) and to move forward with joy. (I was having major episodes of worry with this one. When I finally gave the worrying up to the Universe, in two days the situation got resolved and in a way that was a total surprise.)

- Universe, expose the hypocrisy, the lies that are occurring in our government—regardless of who is doing it—so I can concentrate on my writing instead. (I saw the Universe make this happen every time I made the request.)
- Universe, put people in my path that can help me decide and move forward with my projects. (The Universe did in multiple ways.)

These are just a few examples of my letting go of issues I was worrying and stressing about. It's become a daily practice these days. By letting go, I'm raising my positive vibrations and releasing the stress and the need to worry.

The Law of Vibration is acute and highly attuned. Nothing and no one can escape these vibrations. Everything has vibrational energy—even inanimate objects! It's this vibrational energy that creates our auras[4].

Surround Yourself With Positive People

While trying to raise your own vibrations, it becomes easier to do when you surround yourself with positive people rather than negative ones. We tend to become like those with whom we spend time with.

---

[4] An aura is best described as bubble-like around your entire body. The colors of our auras can change per the energy we give off. It's much like Earth's atmosphere, only an aura is our own personal atmosphere.

This phenomena relates both to the Law of Vibration and the Law of Attraction.

Look for the Lessons

Life happens. Life is about change as much as people don't like or want to change. And, life changes always come with lessons.

The harsher the life event, the bigger the lesson to be learned.

Create New Habits

New habits require repeated behavior or action the same way, same time of day. Think about your morning routine. It's a habit. What do you do with your keys when you come in the door? It's a habit.

The old adage states that if you do something repeatedly for 30 days, it becomes a habit. That old adage is true.

I've been participating in daily Zoom write-ins with other writers six days a week for several months. Sitting down at these specific times has now created a habit. I can now sit down and write during those time periods whether we're online together or not.

Stop the Negativity From Returning

If you're dealing with a negative habit, change your behavior. Substitute. If you want to remove something, you have to insert something else in its place.

Change your routine. Change the time. Change the location. Keep making changes until you can finally break free of that negative behavior, thinking, or reacting.

Just so you know, it's a lot easier to change the thinking than it is the behavior. But, the behavior is what everyone else sees; they can't see how you've changed your thinking.

In Summary

Success isn't just the end result. Success is about the journey, taking the steps. Doing the work day by day. Task by task. Small successes will lead to a greater success. It's about enjoying the journey, because if you're not enjoying the journey, why do it?

Focus on your fire's forward progress no matter how big or small that progress is from day to day or week to week. Celebrate every movement forward and any time you get to spend with your fire.

An example of a journey that could have been swamped because of illness is that of a writer who was dealing with chronic fatigue syndrome. She was asked to write an article about horses but could only write a paragraph or two per day. So obsessed with the article's contents two years after it was published, she began writing a book, while on her back and writing only small bits—a few sentences—day after day. Three years later that book was finished. It became *Seabiscuit: An American Legend*. [5]

A wonderful prime example of how a negative can be turned into a positive.

---

[5] Hillenbrand, Laura. (July 7, 2003). "A Sudden Illness." *The New Yorker*. The entire article about her illness can be viewed here: https://www.newyorker.com/magazine/2003/07/07/a-sudden-illness

DIANA STOUT

CHAPTER 17: Restarting Your Fire

The goal of any physical fire is to obtain coals. Why? Because they can get a fire restarted quickly.

With coals, you can burn the branches and logs because the coals can be so hot internally that they can easily ignite the larger pieces of wood, creating shooting flames again. It's when logs burn that you get coals.

So, how can you get back to where your fire is blazing, providing coals that can ignite when you start a new project, the equivalent of a log?

If the fire has been out or growing cold, *start back slowly*. Try 5-15 minutes a day for a week or more. As your fire grows again, you'll find yourself wanting to spend more time with it. These small chunks of time are your fire starters, which then you can add kindling and logs again.

If the fire is in coals because you've recently finished a major writing project, a new project is easier to start. At the same time, it doesn't hurt to chunk out smaller pieces to get the project going, just so you don't burn yourself out. It's about pacing yourself, keeping the fire steady.

If you know when you want to finish a project, work backwards from that date by writing down smaller task due dates.

If you're willing to meander along with no deadline in mind, you still want to set up some timeline goals. It'll get your fire burning hot again.

Yes, the fire is about passion as it burns hot. But unless the fire is fed, it won't remain hot. So set yourself up to feed your fire on a *regular basis* from week to week. Don't let long periods of time pass by without working on your writing, if you can help it.

Part VII: Protecting Your Fire

"Passion is what gets you through the hardest times."
— Neil deGrasse Tyson

"If you really want to fly, harness your power to your passion."
— Oprah Winfrey

"Twenty years from now you'll be more disappointed by the things you didn't do rather than the ones you did do."
— Mark Twain

CHAPTER 18: Why Your Fire Needs Protection

No one will ever care about your fire more than you.

If you aren't protecting your fire, who is? Who will?

If you're the only one who can protect your fire, who are you protecting it from? The answer is: Everyone who isn't supporting you.

If you're lucky, you'll have family and friends who will support you not only from that first strike of your match but throughout your entire journey, even if it means leaving them behind.

Leaving others behind occurs when

- Your time is now devoted elsewhere, when your availability to meet or chat doesn't match up anymore
- Your daily communications become weekly, monthly, or just once in a while.
- You have to move across the state or across the country, which impacts how often you can get together.
- You realized that one of you is growing to the point that you no longer have that much in

common anymore or that conversations have become difficult because of your differences.

Anyone okay with your fire means they wish you well and recognize that your higher good isn't the same as theirs. That your journeys' paths could be different and even on separate walkways.

When I went to college as a non-traditional student, those in academia cheered me on. Family members and friends looked at me like I had two heads. My best friend at the time told me I was making a huge mistake.

I learned not to talk about it—I had to protect my reasons, which they couldn't understand. I was looking down the road, beyond the headlights . . . to retirement. Their focus was within the headlights, week to week, the upcoming holiday.

Most of these folks had jobs that provided a secure retirement, had jobs that provided benefits of insurance and healthcare options, none of which I had. Teaching would provide those benefits.

For me, it was a win-win, despite the four years I worked and went to school full time before I unexpectedly earned a scholarship that allowed me to quit my office job and teach as a graduate student.

The day I got to quit that day job was the most joyous I'd experienced in a long time. I nearly skipped to the parking lot that last day.

When I received my bachelor's degree, the best compliment came from two women from my day job, who said, "You showed us how to dream and how to get it done."

Stay Away From the Naysayers

While everyone has good intentions, often when people offer advice, they're telling you how to live as it pertains to *their* script.

As a writer, you'll want to associate with other writers, for they are your true support system.

When I was young, I listened to a number of people who were older and had more practical working experience. However, I noticed none of them had passion for their work. It was a job, for pay only.

I wanted more than a job. I wanted the *fire*.

As I found my fire, they expected me to treat it like a hobby. From the beginning, I wanted to earn a living from my writing. Once I started writing in those early days, I always identified myself as a *writer* on my tax returns regardless of what my day job was: clerk, bookkeeper, housewife, bus driver, sales, supervisor, student, professor.

Naysayers tend to see only their path, how they would do things, not realizing how you're not like them.

Those who encourage you can see your emotional, internal need, and generally can see beyond tomorrow. They can see your future as you see it. They might not understand your fire one-hundred percent because it's outside of their life experiences or desires, but they'll be excited for you.

The way to protect your fire from the naysayers is to not let them near your fire. If they can't support you, should they be entitled to know what you're doing? Where they then have availability to throw water (their negativity) on the fire?

The answer is a resounding No. Protect your fire.

That said, it's possible that you could be the one destroying your fire.

Protecting Your Fire From Yourself

In recognizing that I wanted to be a writer, naturally I couldn't ignore my kids and any job I had.

This was where I had to examine my life more closely, at how I spent my time in a typical week. Events I attended. Hobbies. Time with other people. This is where I made some major changes about how I spent my time.

I learned I couldn't say yes to everything as I once had. If I volunteered, that would be time taken away from my writing. Also, I knew if I did say *yes*, I would soon feel resentful that I had.

Do we say yes because we're afraid they won't be friends with us anymore if we say *no*? If that's true, what are we really losing?

Lots of positive self-talk was required during this period of time as I made changes.

The bottom line in protecting your fire is to simply be aware of the dangers that can snuff it out. Dangers that can come from any direction, including yourself.

DIANA STOUT

CHAPTER 19: Dealing With Regrets

One thing many people say when finding out that I'm a writer is: *I've always wanted to write.*

Me: *So, why don't you?*

The excuses I hear most often are:

- I'm too old
- I wouldn't be any good.
- I don't have an education.

Age is not relevant. Desire is. You're never too old. Age is only an obstacle if *you* make it one.

Not being any good isn't relevant. Wanting to learn is. We're all unpracticed when we begin anything new. Practice creates expertise.

Not having an education? A doable fix.

The spoken regrets I've heard:

I regret not going to college. This has been said by a number of individuals, some as young as 30 and others as old as 60. When I respond that it's never too late to go back to school, the next response is, *I don't have the time.* Or, *I don't have the money.*

When I tell them that I once believed the same thing but discovered both to be untrue, and with today's online colleges, getting a college education is far easier than it used to be. They just stare at me, which tells me while yes, they have the regret, they're also not interested in doing the work.

I regret not moving away. When asked why they didn't when they had the chance, *fear* was the number one answer. Worry accompanied that fear; they worried they wouldn't get a job or one that would pay enough, that they wouldn't make any new friends. They let their fear box them in.

I regret not pursuing my own interests. When asked further, I learned they were living a life some else had mapped out for them: a parent, a sibling, a spouse. They wanted to avoid conflict.

I regret not learning how to play the piano. That particular musical instrument above all others is most named. When I reveal that I started taking piano lessons when I was 25 and pregnant, that age doesn't matter, the new excuses are about not having the time or money.

I was willing to make sacrifices elsewhere so that I could learn how to play, and I don't regret those sacrifices one bit.

If you want something badly enough, you'll make the effort. You'll do the work. You'll expend the energy.

From the article, "Nurse Reveals 5 Most Common Regrets People Have Before They Die," these are the top regrets people have said when facing death.[6] They wished that they had:

- lived the life they had always wanted, not what others wanted for them.
- worked fewer hours, spent more time with families.
- been able to state their feelings about everything, both good and bad.
- stayed connected with others, especially friends.
- allowed themselves to not just be content but had allowed themselves the ability to let go of unhappiness and to be happy, instead.

Do you have any regrets? If so, what are they? What's the excuse you used to not pursue it/them?

Would it surprise you to learn that you can change these regrets to actions? Even now?

There isn't anything you can't do, *if* you want to do it badly enough.

---

[6] Soleil, Valerie, B.A., LL.B. May 20, 2016. Website: https://www.learning-mind.com/common-regrets-people-have-before-they-die/ Retrieved September 26, 2021.

DIANA STOUT

Part VIII: The Final Test

"Believe in yourself and all that you are. Know that there is something inside you that is greater than any obstacle."

        Christian D. Larson, author & teacher

"The Greeks didn't write obituaries. Instead, they asked just one question: did he have passion?"

        – from the movie, *Serendipity*

DIANA STOUT

CHAPTER 20: Final Assignment

You didn't think I was going to forget about all those assignments you've done over the course of this book, did you?

Returning to each of those assignments, now that you're almost finished reading this book and have been thinking about your fire and where you're at in the building of that fire, let's take a look at those lists and comments.

They'll help you evaluate changes you want to make and help give your fire shape and promise. As your fire burns over time, you'll change and so will the width and depth of your fire.

So, here we go, looking at each assignment individually:

Chapter 4's Success Assignment – Does the fire you're creating satisfy your definition of success, or are you finding you want to rewrite that definition?

Chapter 5's Why Assignment: Has your *Why* evolved or has it remained the same? Does your *Why* make you smile and warm your heart?

Chapter 5's Passion Assignment: What's happened to

that list? Have you dropped some activities? Relegated some to a bucket list? Are you turning some into simple hobbies when not working on your fire? Did any of them become your fire?

Chapter 6's Passion Quotient Evaluation Assignment: Has your Passion Quotient number gone up? Or, did you realize you may have rated it too high in the beginning?

Chapter 14's Worry, Anxiety, Stress Assignment: Are you discovering areas of your life where you can lessen or let go of previous worries, anxiety, or stress? Are you noticing where you can make changes, which will help you improve your life, moving your further into positivity?

The Final Evaluation

What is your final take-away now that you've evaluated the assignments, found your fire, or have assessed its current heat level.

What's been most helpful in reading this book? What new ideas have you gleaned?

Is your fire what you thought it would be?

Are you surprised by the potential growth you can now see for your fire? Where you can build it bigger and better than it ever has been before?

Are you recognizing the value of the three different

types of fire fuel that you can apply to your fire: the tinder, kindling, and main fuel and when to apply each?

DIANA STOUT

CHAPTER 21: In Conclusion

My fire—that passion the Greeks are talking about in their obituaries—is what drives me through the rough times.

Success doesn't happen overnight for most people. Yes, the lucky ones we hear and read about inspire our own dreams and desires. But reality for most of us means plugging away at our passions day by day.

I'm still reaching and striving for some of those goals: becoming a best-selling author and getting a script produced.

The uplifting news is even if I never obtain the title of best-selling author or get to see my work on the screen—big or small—I will have achieved something far greater. I learned how to write, publish, and connect with other writers and teachers who understand the importance of words. I enjoyed my journey because I fed my fire, thus allowing me to explore, deliver, and live my passion.

I got to enjoy the passion of the journey.

My writing, my fire, is something I own alone. No one else controls it.

My fire reduced my stress through life and it still does.

My fire allows me to keep learning, something I fully enjoy.

My fire keeps me connected to others like myself. They're my tribe and always will be no matter where I go or where I may move in the future.

My fire keeps me doing and practicing. I continue to learn and improve.

Recently, when someone asked me why I was smiling all the time, I responded, "Because I'm happy." Their response was, "But you're not married, not even in a relationship. You live in a small apartment."

I just smiled.

Life is about choices and changes.

So what choices and changes are you willing to make?

What's your fire?

ABOUT THE AUTHOR

Diana Stout, MFA, Ph.D. is an award-winning screenwriter, author, and former English professor whose writing led her into academic teaching. Her students would say, "She smiles when she talks about writing." Published in multiple genres, she enjoys helping other writers learn the craft.

When not writing, she enjoys reading, rainy days, movies, watching birds at her feeders, gardening, jigsaw puzzles, and visiting with family and friends.

To learn more about Diana, visit the following:

Website: sharpenedpencilsproductions.com
Facebook: facebook.com/writerDianaStout
Twitter: twitter.com/ScreenWryter13
Pinterest: pinterest.com/drdianastout
Instagram: instagram.com/authordianastout
BookBub: bookbub.com/authors/diana-stout
Goodreads: goodreads.com/user/show/43124185-diana-stout

Blogs

Behind the Scenes – life as a writer dianastout.net
Into the Core – life as an intuitive: dianastout.com
Behind the Scenes with Diana Stout & Featured Guests dianastout.org

Can You Help Me, Please?

Can you leave a quick review?

Providing a review is the best way for a reader to thank the author.

Reviews can be short!
- I loved this book!
- I like this book!
- I couldn't put this book down!

It's not the length of a review that counts; it's the number of reviews that a book gets that counts.

THANK YOU!

Join My Facebook Group

Want to join others like yourself who are finding their fire, have started their fire, or are reaping the rewards of tending to their fire?

Those who have read any of my books are welcome my Facebook group, Dr. Diana's Creative Warriors. While you may think the group is only for writers, it's for anyone who reads my how-to books where they've found this link, readers who want to become better versions of themselves. To join, go to his Facebook group, which cannot be searched or seen. You can only gain access via this URL. Be sure to answer *all* of the questions.
https://www.facebook.com/groups/1154207845314046

Coming soon!

The working title for the next book in this how-to series is:

Time Management for Writers (and everyone else, too)

Based on exercises and methods developed for myself and students in my workshops, this book will show you how to find extra time that you want to devote to your writing, to your fire.

To stay informed and be notified when the book comes

out, subscribe to my newsletter!
http://www.subscribepage.com/x5k2t9

I promise not to fill your mailbox, emailing you only on occasion when I have freebies to offer or when I have announcements of new books coming out.

www.ingramcontent.com/pod-product-compliance
Lightning Source LLC
Chambersburg PA
CBHW050434010526
44118CB00013B/1527